DINOSAUR BONES

by the same author

Swan Dive

Music of the Spheres

Out of Mind

DINOSAUR BONES

POEMS

MICHAEL BURKE

PARLOR PRESS
Anderson, South Carolina
www.parlorpress.com

Parlor Press LLC, Anderson, South Carolina, 29621

Printed in the United States of America
S A N: 2 5 4 - 8 8 7 9

Library of Congress Cataloging-in-Publication Data on File

Names: Burke, Michael, 1939- author.
Title: Dinosaur bones : poems / Michael Burke.
Description: Anderson, South Carolina : Parlor Press, [2021] | Summary: "Dinosaur Bones collects poems written by Michael Burke over his career as an acclaimed visual artist. "-- Provided by publisher.
Identifiers: LCCN 2020046501 (print) | LCCN 2020046502 (ebook) | ISBN 9781643171876 (paperback ; acid-free paper) | ISBN 9781643171883 (pdf) | ISBN 9781643171890 (epub)
Subjects: LCGFT: Poetry.
Classification: LCC PS3602.U75525 D56 2021 (print) | LCC PS3602. U75525 (ebook) | DDC 811/.6--dc23
LC record available at https://lccn.loc.gov/2020046501
LC ebook record available at https://lccn.loc.gov/2020046502

978-1-64317-187-6 (paperback)
978-1-64317-188-3 (PDF)
978-1-64317-189-0 (ePub)

2 3 4 5

Book design by David Blakesley.
All illustrations throughout this book were created by Michael Burke.
Cover art by Michael Burke.
Printed on acid-free paper.

Parlor Press, LLC is an independent publisher of scholarly and trade titles in print and multimedia formats. This book is available in paperback and ebook formats from Parlor Press on the World Wide Web at http://www.parlorpress.com or through online and brick-and-mortar bookstores. For submission information or to find out about Parlor Press publications, write to Parlor Press, 3015 Brackenberry Drive, Anderson, South Carolina, 29621, or email editor@parlorpress.com.

for Julie, Shannon and Brendan

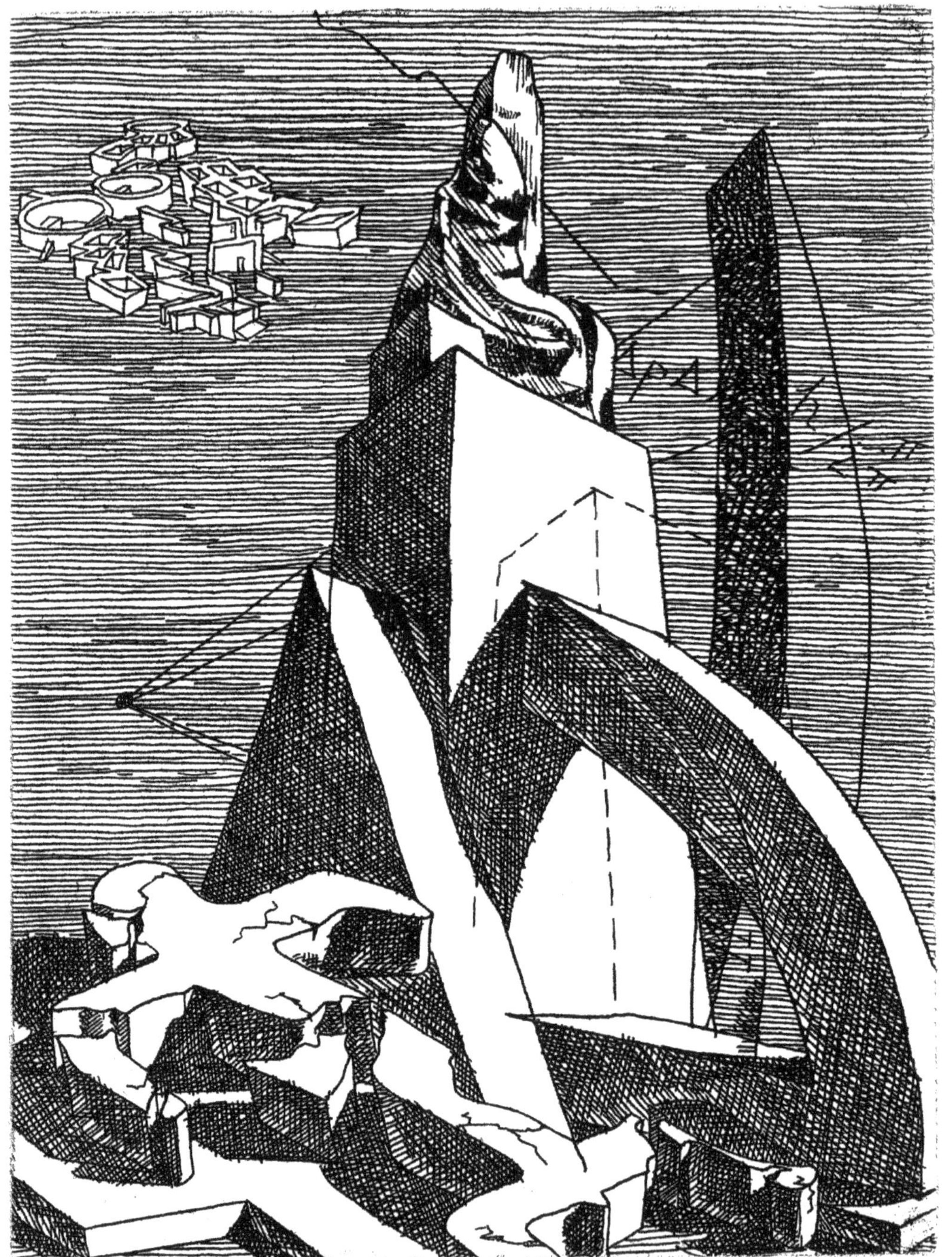

CONTENTS

SONNETS

POEMS FOR THE SUMMER SOLSTICE

PREFACE

Poems I have written over many years. From long to short, serious to lighthearted, literal to abstract. They were inspired by past loves, past losses, fantasies, hopes and strange fears. From times I hope you will recall, to experiences that I feel are solely mine.

It is troubling though that in the last year the world has been turned upside down – by a virus that moves with incredible speed and by important issues that have occurred for too many years before being taken seriously, Black Lives Matter.

I hope you can read the poems and feel emotions you have experienced, even though you are bombarded by our ever-changing present. I've tried writing poems that reflect the present, and have found it impossible. I've tried to shrink the distance between then and now, with the hope that it engages the thoughts of the present and hope for the future.

DINOSAUR BONES

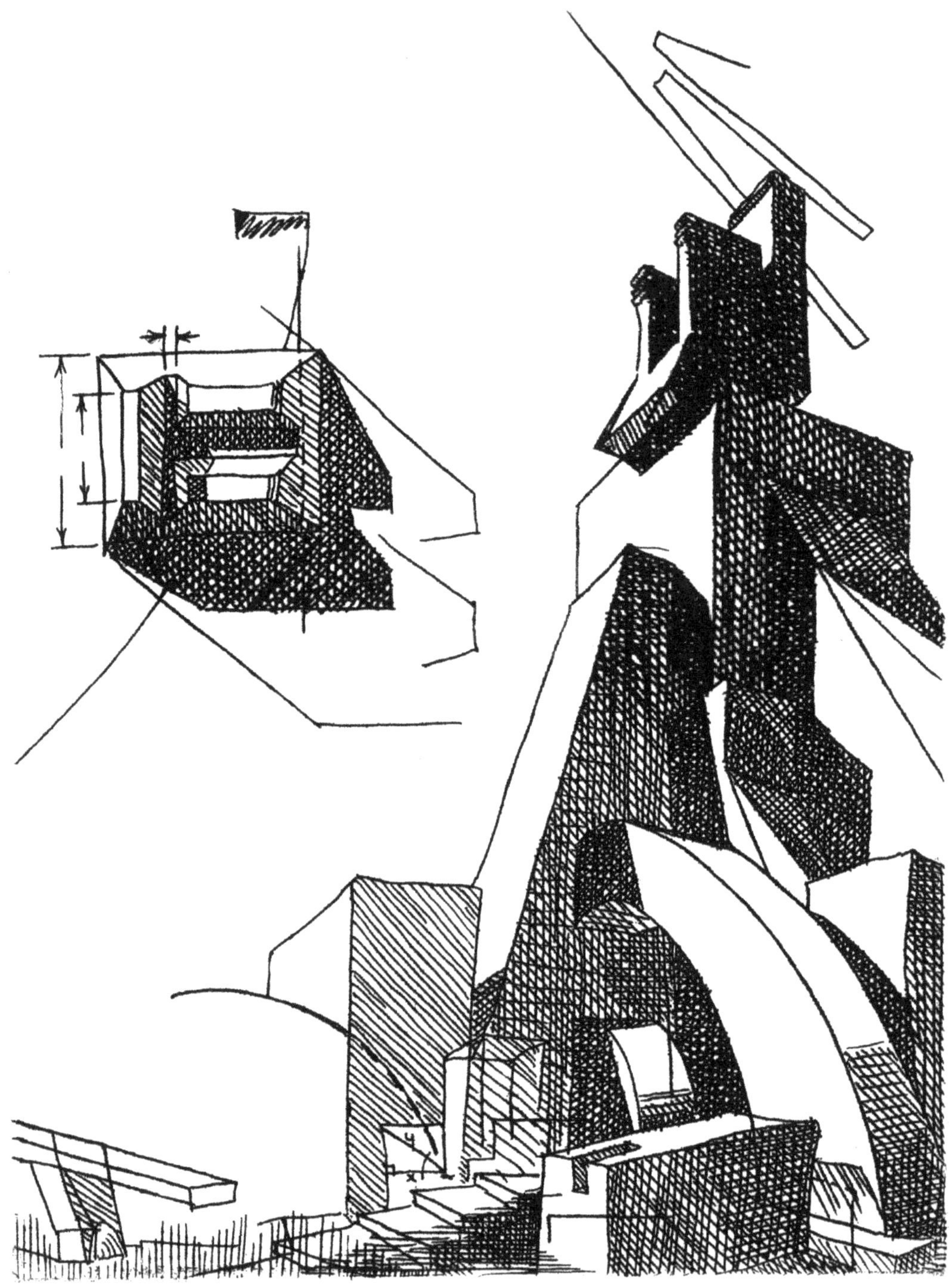

CATERPILLARS DON'T WRITE POEMS

Caterpillars don't write poems
Birds write poems

They soar above us
Float, swoop, dive
Glory in the sun
Glow in the colors of its rising and setting
And become a piece of the wind

Caterpillars struggle along
Under dead leaves
Meeting slugs and ants

Rolled into a ball to escape attention
Squashed underfoot
Patterned to avoid the sharp vision of the bird poet

To be prey to a poet – what worse fate

Run caterpillar run
Faster
One foot after another, and another, and another
Don't trip

A life on the ground is the fate of the old
We age from butterfly to caterpillar

With memories of the view of mountains
Storms that were seen in the distance
Warnings given
To guard against heavy feet
Slogging through the mud
In the rain

WORDS

Dim, in the early morning light
I may have imagined
A firefly
A glow
A growing shaft of light
Forcing a path through a crack in the plaster over my bed
Breaking free, a bright burst of light
Sprinkled with flecks, like pepper
Which, as they fell closer, became letters
ABC's scattering over the bedcovers
And about the wooden floor
The gravel of thought, crunching underfoot
Scurrying to form into words
Sentences to quote
Stories that I could tell
If only they would stay in focus

These words hide everywhere in our house
In the books
Hundreds of books
Every wall a shelf of books
Recent books lying on top of the dusty standing old-timers

Lying on the table, by the fireplace
The fat Merriam-Webster
It's pages revealingly spread
To display the last word searched for
The final word to settle any dispute
Each thing in the house became first, the word
Chair – one word, but so many chairs;
Big, small, old, wooden, broken...
Carpet – noun, adverb, adjective
They carpet bombed the carpet baggers, thus destroying the carpets
Tree – branches, twigs, prickly fruit, falling leaves, green now, orange later
Lonely sounds when the fall wind blows through the dry leaves

Tree – I once fell out of a maple, with a saw in my hand
Landed in leaves
But cut my wrist, leaving a scar
It caused an awkward silence in group therapy
Awkward silence, but what other kind is there
Frozen, tongue-tied
Papered over with silly words

Words to explain words, but some resisted
Neurosis, sublimation, transference
Definitions that remained in fog

I was attacked once by a stream of words
Meaningless, but solid and sharp
Laced with invective
I was quiet – words didn't come easily
But I knew that the best words were the ones I wasn't supposed to say
– Bad words, curse words, soap on the tongue words

My friend in fifth grade, Crazy Johnny
Yelled curses in church
Until they grabbed him
Threw him out the side door
Where he had to stay,
Outside, all alone
In the sun

THE MUSIC OF THE SPHERES

(for Julie)

I cannot hear Julie
Over the din of Ninth Avenue
When she speaks to me as we walk
She has the voice of the desert
Grown in the quiet of Utah
The voice of Europe
Where no TV played in the cafés
The quiet drawn out accent of the southwest
Made musical by teaching English to executives
Blowing glass in a factory near Paris
A small upswing at the end of each sentence
To establish the propriety of the English language
Connie asks: "would you like a cup of tea?"
Tee – ee; two syllables, rising
She speaks as though I were a spirit floating around her
My ear fluttering in front
Ready to intercept the waves of sound
No matter what direction they are sent
Questions remain un-heard and unanswered

If I could see the cones of sound
Like ripples on a lake
I could read them into words
And from the pile, falling loosely in the brain
I could build sentences
Like astronomers who peer into the sky
Hearing sounds
Made fourteen million years ago

Once, I saw sounds
During the summer solstice
In The Philharmonic Hall in St. Petersburg
The sun of the white nights, refusing to set
Bounced along the rooftops
Peeking in and out from behind the peaks and chimneys
It shown not down upon us
As in lower latitudes
Where it made one feel important
Here, in the North, the rays glance off the edge of the earth
On their way to constellations yet un-named
The sunlight, strangely pale at 10 in the evening
Moves parallel to the ground
Streams in the high windows over our heads
Shimmering the glass facets of the chandeliers into
Blue-yellow-red spectrums scattered about the hall

The magic white light of June
Sun in the late evening
Mixes uncomfortably with the formal black tie orchestra
As they lift their instruments
The overture begins
Ripples of sound rise into the hall
Where each pulse jiggles the glass jewels hanging above
The refracted light beams now become the messengers of the music
I watch
As a tiny rainbow vibrates in rhythm on Julie's bare neck
In tune, with the music

PERSPECTIVE

(for Shannon)

We would walk a mile on the dirt road
Stopping along the way at a rocky cut in the earth
The old New Jersey iron mine
Revived by the need for Civil War cannons
Now dead again, covered over with the fast-growing red maples
That, without the forest fires to help the oaks and
With blights that stopped the chestnuts and elms
Are taking over the land
And paying their way with a fall spectacle

Over a hundred years ago the hillside was stripped
The trees were cleared and burned in pits
To make the charcoal that would burn hot enough to melt the ore
Separating the good from the bad
The iron was carried by horse cart
Along the country road where we walked
To the railroad
A high embankment had been built, to keep the tracks level
As they ran straight through the valley
A mile from our house
The goal of our afternoon walk

My father, my mother, my brother and I
Left the dirt road where it went through the culvert
We climbed up the bric-a-brac
Yard wide coal-like rocks
Piled rudely over a field, and through a piece of the Wolf Lake swamp
To carry the single pair of iron rails
Laid over thousands of ties
Square-cut chestnut
Soaked black with creosote, they would never rot
They made a good foundation for our outhouse

The fabulous track
The only straight line amidst nature's curves and chaos
Without the least waver, as far as one could see
Towards the West it disappeared into a dark hole in the mountain
And to the East it ran straight seemingly forever
The two lines merging into one
Giving me my first notion of the power of the vanishing point
Knowing full well, that the two tracks never came together

As the light of the long summer's day began to soften
As my brother and I balanced ourselves on the bars
        Rusted steel, shined only along the top by metal wheels
The rails would start to sing
A high pitched harmonic, floating without a source
And we knew that the train to Chicago,
With it's dining cars, and sleeping cars
        Was approaching as it did every evening

Our mother would see it first
Perhaps because she was higher, and could see farther around the curve of the Earth
We squinted to the East to find the dot of black
The vanishing point that had become real
Motionless, with no speed, no shape
Betrayed by the changing pitch of the singing rail
Now it seemed, complaining a bit

Slowly, the dot developed edges
A partly imagined shape, the circle over the triangle cow-catcher
        As it appeared in our children's books
On the horizon, the front of a tiny engine formed
The angel's song from the rail was replaced by a low rhythm
Chugging from the pistons,
        We could see the smoke

Then, it seemed without warning
The engine raced at us with increasing speed
As though we were lying on our backs
Watching a train falling from the sky, accelerating, upon us
Faster, speed by square and distance
The acceleration that Newton described
Not with the apple from the tree
But with the invention of a language to see by
The notion of calculus, the means to deal with points
That are always changing, no matter how finely divided

There was just time to jump from the tracks
Or so we imagined by standing just a bit too long on the rails
Before the iron horse crashed by
With a roar
And a whistle that dropped off Doppler's cliff
The pressure of sound and air as it passed
Was enough to blow one from the narrow edge

Lit windows flickered by
Like images on an old nickelodeon comedy
Flashes of heads
Most unconcerned with us, while reading a newspaper, or dozing
A few, looking out, imagined a life to fit the quick glimpse of a small staring boy
Gone in a second
As I stared out the window
Returning on the train from Chicago, where my daughter stayed
In the middle of the college quadrangle
With cruel bagpipes playing
We hugged and she walked in one direction never looking back
And I in the other, looking back again and again
As she got smaller
Shrinking to the size of a child, then to a baby, and to a vanishing point

THE NEW YEAR

(for Brendan)

My studio is on the 7th floor
The building is plain garment industry industrial – 1920s
Only right angles
Or, as experience has taught
Angles that are close to right angles
Say, between about 86 to 94 degrees
But never exactly a right angle

The ceiling; 11 feet 2 inches
Or in some places 11 feet l, or 11
Defines the size of my sculpture
One piece is 11 feet 1 ½ inches high
And can stand only in one place
Near the windows that face south

Or actually 7 degrees off true south, I think it's 7
Or 7.2 degrees, depending on the millennium
For the earth tilts back and forth, every 50 thousand years or so
And the magnetic pole wanders around the top of the sphere
Which isn't really round anyway
Sort of pear-shaped in truth
A fact which became obvious when the first satellite
Didn't appear to follow a circle
Or, more accurately, an ellipse

So how old does that make me?
65—give or take a bit.
An age that has no astronomical correlation
No syzygy, no alignment in the heavens
But neither does the New Year, which puzzles me
The date when all is renewed
When the calendar ends
And begins again
Does not line up with anything
As a solstice, or an equinox

Today, on the first day of the New Year
The shadow of the edge of the window
At 11:05 am
Just touches the tip of my sleeping cat's tail
Before it twitches
Starting a line
From tail to window sill to sun
About 93.6 million miles, roughly one astronomical unit

A straight line that exists for an infinitesimal moment
And is as elusive
As the comings and goings of my son
Who leaves a path
Which may, or may not
Intersect with mine

BEETLES BEWARE

I walk looking down

As tho to avoid crushing insects underfoot

This allows me to become invisible

Hiding to keep from being found out

All the while, dreaming

Of being discovered

Now, I will gaze parallel to the earth

Noticed by others

As I stride ahead

Beetles, seeing me coming,

Scramble for their lives.

I MADE A LIST

I made a list once
Of all the vehicles I ever drove
Anything that had a motor was included

Cars and trucks
Mowers, tractors, and a backhoe
Airplanes, boats, motorcycles, gliders
No, the glider doesn't count, no motor

I was lucky for having never killed anyone, or
Unless I've blocked it out
Hurt some innocent

But I did run over a woodchuck once, late at night
And swore uncharacteristically, frightening Mabel
Who probably caused the whole thing
By making me promise never to touch
Her breast again
I was thinking of facing a lifetime without Mabel's breast
Didn't see the woodchuck

Mostly I was pretty sane behind the wheel, no road rage
Although once, when I was an astronomer, I did get a bit crazy
Driving down Haleakala
A two-mile high volcano in Hawaii

Perhaps the thin air at the observatory
Ten thousand feet above the Pacific
Had lightened my brain

Perhaps it was the unreality of watching
The satellite 22,000 miles above
Speed around the earth
To return every 90 minutes

But when the stars faded
And the sun arose
Frances took the pick-up
I drove the station wagon
We started down
20 miles of switchbacks on the side of the volcano,
And began to race.
Not each other really,
Just time, or life, or good sense

I skidded on gravel around one turn
And took out a green and yellow park sign
I think it said "dangerous curve ahead"

But we kept on
The metal around the lug nuts on the pick-up couldn't take the stress
Frances' rear tire sheared off the rim
We skidded to a stop

The tire bounced over the edge, and
Started down the steep slope of the volcano
Rolling over the lava, into the meadow
Then disappearing into the eucalyptus woods
3,000 feet below

Our tire, now out of sight, was bounding on
Free, happy, reckless
Through the pineapple fields, then the sugar cane
It exploded at the beach and dove into the Pacific
Sinking four miles down

The metal rim came to rest near a deep-sea vent
Where there is no oxygen
Where creatures breathe sulphur
Where life on earth may have begun

We have travelled from the very specific
From Mabel's breast
To the infinite reaches of the universe
And back to the unknown depths of the sea

Where
A future aquanaut will arrive
See the metal rim and think
"Aha, those carbon-based sulpher-breathing creatures drove cars"

Then he will smile, and think of
Frances and me
Sitting on the edge of the mountain road
Laughing, and laughing, and laughing

MYSTERIOUS STUFF

There was a small room under the eaves
Guarded by a low wooden door
Good for keeping out the grown-ups
And we had filled it with mysterious stuff

Well, mostly my older brother did
He saved tubes and condensers and resistors
Coils of wire, and toggle switches
Scavenged from grandfather's broken radios

He labeled them with a secret code of letters and numbers
Packed them in cigar boxes
And arranged them in rows on unpainted shelves

Starting with a metal skeleton
Left over from an art deco electronic device
While wielding a soldering iron
He built machines
Sculptures of metal and glass, that glowed and hummed
Justified by uses unexplained to me

A spark machine that I wasn't allowed to touch
An oscilloscope built into an old wooden cabinet
A crystal set which crackled with static
When we took it to the back porch
Aimed the antenna in the direction of the city
Listening for sounds to arrive over the curve of the earth

I had a softball
A small earth with laces like mountain ridges
I tossed it up and caught it a thousand times

The fingers of my baseball mitt were tied together with leather laces
It was too big for a child's hand
For it was given to me by my cousin Arthur
He told us stories of World War II
When he flew in a B-24 as a bombardier

I could throw my softball higher than the fir in the yard
Higher even than the elm tree
Which had survived the blight,
Because it stood apart from other trees

From my brother's physics book I learned that
If a ball were thrown high enough, and fast enough,
In the direction of the mountain
Beyond the garden
It would sail into orbit
Traveling above and around the earth

THREE VIEWS OF ANONYMITY

I

I squeeze past someone, in the tight aisle
Between tables, piled with magazines
Stacked bare bodies and faces
In two dimensions,

On a slick page she lies with a stranger
Whose beads of sweat are crisp in detail
She is staring at the almost naked man's socks
Thinking she has seen them hanging from a line
Somewhere in a warm breeze

She left a mother
Alive
And a father
In a room with rugs and a low ceiling and photographs
Of grandmothers and grandfathers
Of uncles and cousins.

II

We shall name her Neutrino
For she passes through
Makes no fuss
Creates no trail
Disturbs no one,
Unmeasurable, with no appreciable mass
No electrical charge
She is powered by the strong force, the weak force,
Sugar, caffeine, and cocaine

She can be heard
Only by ears sunk deep in polar ice
To help their concentration
and avoid ringing phones

She can be remembered only by a chance collision
With Proton, in a cloudy chamber
The baby Muon will carry the builder's plans and mistakes
Leaving gods in the gravel of broken asteroids
And devils in the crumbs of a croissant

III

She grew up as the third child of the bog man
Whose skull we sawed in the lab
She used to draw on the walls
With burnt charcoal
Her favorite bison posed sideways in the meadow

The spirals stood for love
The squares for the secret hide-out by the large circle of stones
Her father said they were left by people who were no more than beasts
She and I pretended it was a machine
That came from the sky
But when the sun went dark, I ran away
Leaving only my footprints in the concrete
And my quarters in the slots
Of the peepshows in Times Square

DINOSAUR BONES

I

I learned to love the dinosaurs
When they were only bones,
Bleached white
They lay quietly in bits and pieces
Under dusty museum glass
In poor light

This dinosaur once rested in soft tar
And remained, until
Its bones were spooned from the earth
By men who love their trade
Labeled, cleaned, polished
Reassembled in a ladder of ribs
Each, a smaller copy of the one before
At the top, a naked skull
Looked down, at me
Standing alone
For my friends had stayed outside, to play ball on the grass
And picnic beneath the sun

I am older now,
The museum is clean, brightly painted,
Nylon grass carpets the display
The bones are hidden
Under mylar skin stretched on aluminum frames
Taut, like fabric on the wings of a biplane
New dinosaurs stand, threatening
In high spaces, where they cast no shadows
On the crowds assembled in wide aisles
Who've come to mingle with history
In its new finery

II

I wander in the junkyards
At night
Out of hearing
To yell to the dark of the beauty
Of the gritty steel bones
In the black drawbridges of the Pulaski Skyway
Lit by methane torches
That burn atop the refineries
Each metal rib
Holds another in place

I call my complaints upwards
Into the sky over limestone footprints
The waves of sound rise into the night
Strike first the face of the moon
And return

On a computer screen
In a room with twinkling lights
My reflections are mixed with the incoming sounds of a pulsar
Who spoke at the moment when dinosaurs lived
Together we are captured in the data
Conspiring to distort the curve
And add a few inches to the distance to the moon

III

When it comes to telling time
I prefer to hide inside the clock
To lecture on the charm of the gears, cogs, and springs
As I look out, through the face
The hands move counter-clockwise
Rolling up time like a window blind

When I was young
My brother and I found some bones
Mixed with pine needles
Near the kerosene drums
In the field behind our house
We threw away pieces of the leathery skin
And clumpy bits of fur
And soaked the bones in bleach
Very fine, precise
We tried to recreate the tiny fingers
He was, perhaps, a raccoon
Or an opossum, playing dead

POLAR - BIPOLAR

I went to the dentist the other day
And this is what he had to say
To try to explain the pain away

X-rays and probes, he looked me over
And said I had an infected molar
I said, actually, I'm bipolar

I'm really telling you the truth
It's not a problem with my tooth

The earth is headed north to south
My mind is headed south to north
The problem is not in my mouth
It's my brain, the troubled source

I'm anxious on bright summer days
I'd often like to be not me
A dentist won't send the pain away
The answer is, a dry martini

THE MARTINI TRIPTYCH

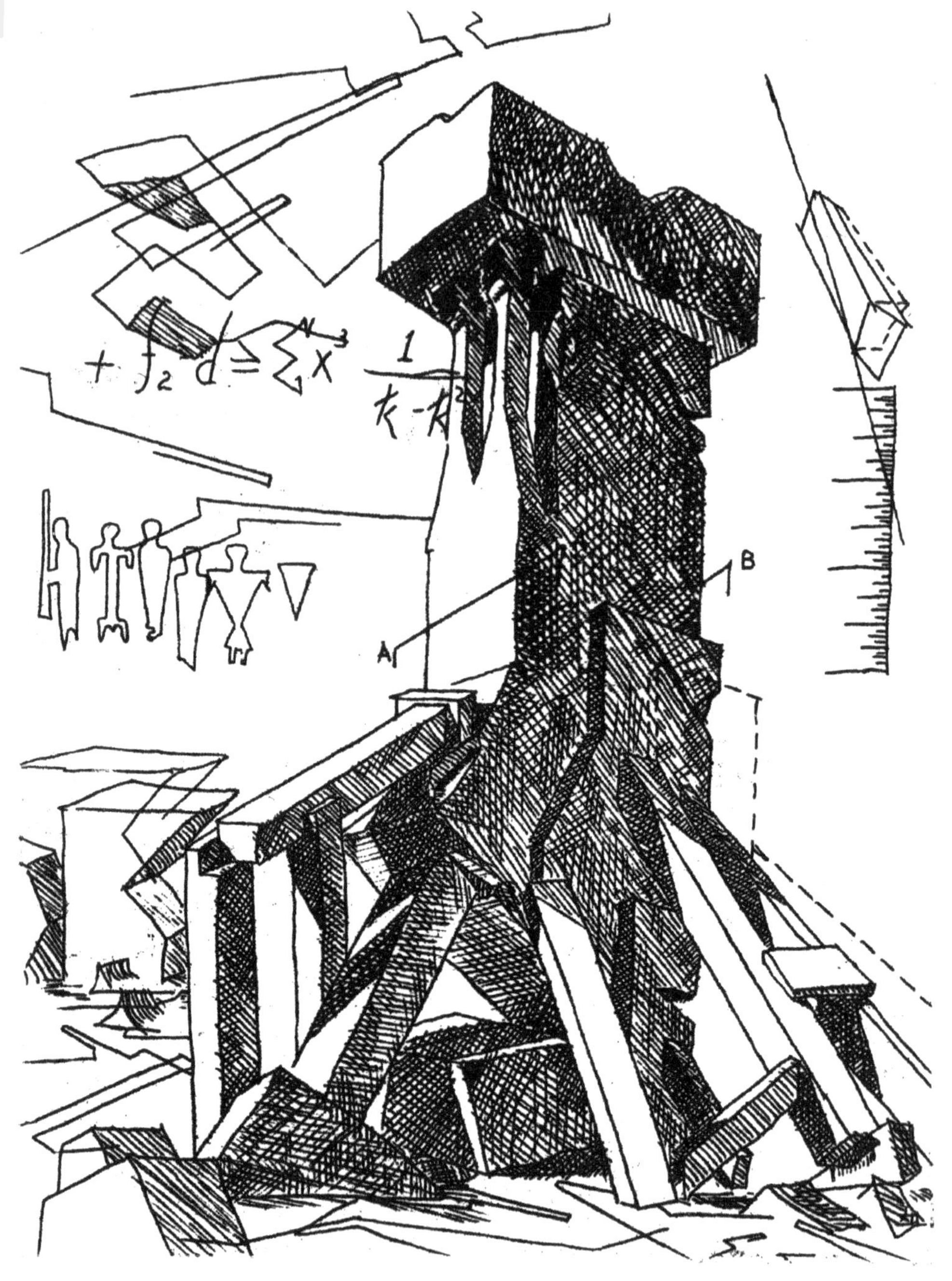
B
A

1. I KNOW I'M GETTING OLDER, BECAUSE

I know I'm getting older
Because:
I talk to myself
I tell myself what I am doing:
"Hmmm – I'm thirsty," I say. "Guess I'll get a martini."
And then I hum a bit,
On the way to the fridge.

I know I'm getting older
Because:
On the street I get a curious look,
Like, 'were you talking to me?'
But there are advantages to getting older,
On the street,
On the crowded streets and subways and busses

Because:
I can smile at a young woman
And she smiles back – I'm no threat
Just a pleasant face
And maybe she feels good about it
I do

I do worry a bit, though,
Because:
Maybe, in the future
Maybe, in the near future
I might talk to myself when people are listening,
When my grown up children can hear me

Already, I watch for the spies on the street,
The camera in the elevator,
The microphone in the park,
In the trees
In the bushes
In my salad.

Well, that was just a notion that I thought would amuse me
So I say it out loud:
"Hi there, salad"
And then, I am at a loss for words

2. DRINKING ALONE

I used to think that I would never drink alone
A beer with friends
A martini on the deck, or two
Some conversation, some laughter
Maybe, even, a few insults, but who's counting

I never knew what it was like to be alone

Lonely, yes.
You weren't invited to the – what was it
A birthday party,
A getting together among friends
But they were always there, somewhere
Talking about me

Now they aren't there
Not laughing at some party
So maybe another martini is okay
It helps me laugh at the jokes on the TV

And remember
Standing,
On stage,
In the lights
Lights so bright I cannot see the audience

But they applaud,
They cheer,
And a voice in the back calls for an encore

3. I HAVE A QUESTION

I have a question
In my last two poems the word martini has appeared
Why is that?

What lovely simile
Beautiful summation
Remarkable insight
Requires the word martini?

Why do thoughts of the cosmos, of love, of life
Of age, of loss, of promise,
Need to be viewed through a glass?

The answer is the glass,
The long, thin stem,
The perfect inverted cone
The balanced sip from the brim

It is the discussion
This gin or that
Bombay Sapphire versus Hendricks
Shaken or stirred
I like mine with ice
Dry or....
I'm sorry, dry is the only option
Vermouth is the enemy of a fine martini

Enemies, and memories
That's why martinis are important
He used to be my friend
I wasn't invited
She never called

The gin is the spark of life
Vermouth, the Puritan caution
Memories melt with the ice cubes

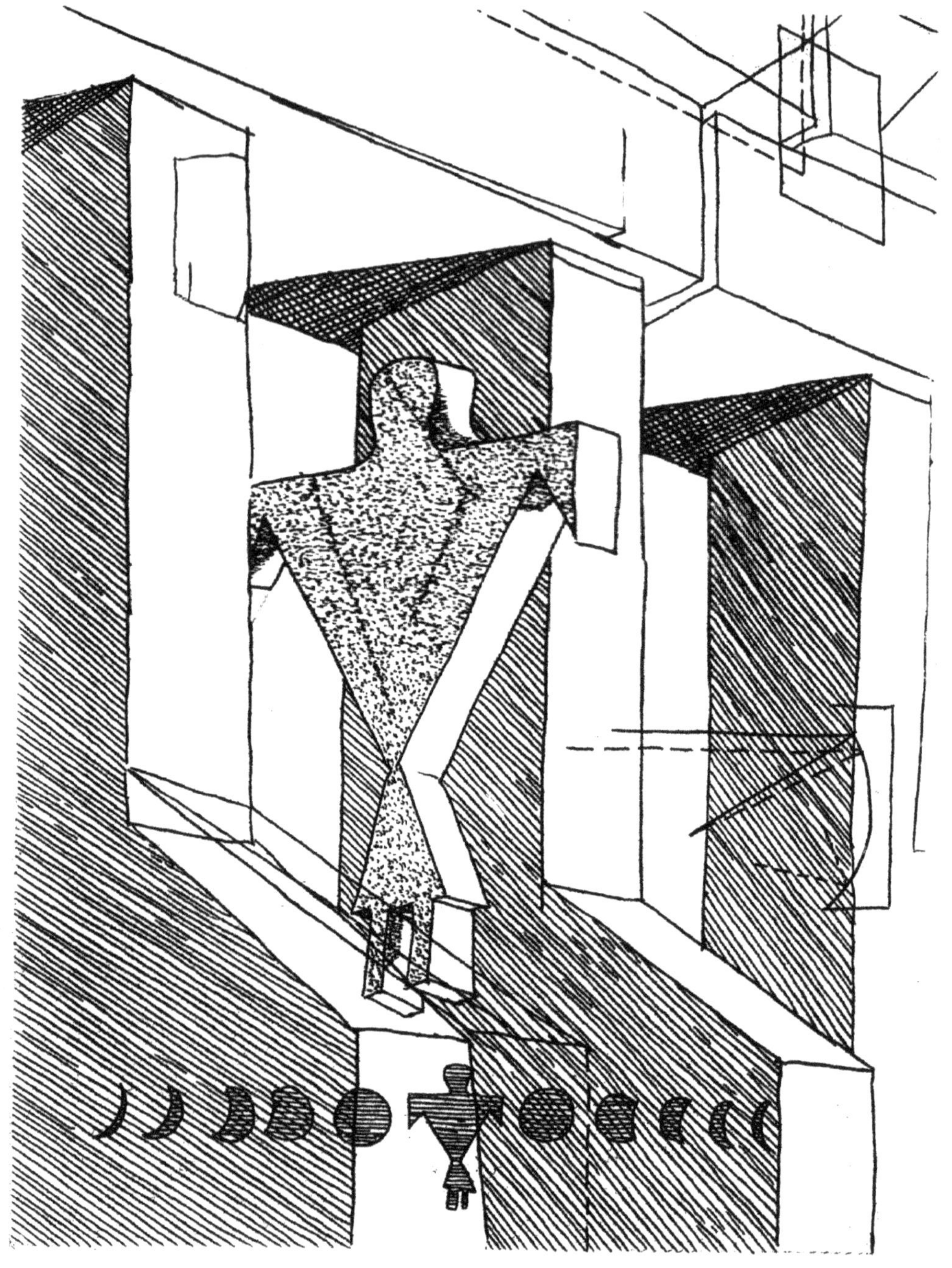

OBSERVERS

It is the suicide hour
The others are asleep
While I roam our loft,
Chew on salt-free crackers, and
Censor thoughts, and
Search my brain for a green field
Where I can picture myself stretched out and dreaming

Through the glass of my seventh floor window, which faces north
A reflected figure faces me
I look through him to 37th street
To a man standing by the dumpster
His head tilted slightly upwards

I check my son's breathing, and return
The man hasn't moved
Nor has my reflection
Or the silhouette in a 12th floor window
A block farther north

In Heisenberg's uncertainty, there are no anonymous observers
The event behaves as a particle, when watched from here
And as a wave, when watched from there
Alone, it is, in all probabilities, both

The street is vacant
He has left, I didn't see him go
And the high window is also empty
Were they part of my experiment
Or I, of theirs?
Without looking back
My reflection, now tired, moves away

He didn't sleep well last night
He lay awake, half-dreaming
Worrying about the calamities
    That could befall his children
In the morning
    He took refuge in the streets
    Walking in the concrete anonymity of the city

Thinking that all streets were one way
    He stepped in front of a moving car
Jumping forward, he stood for an instant
    Between two speeding sedans
    A bearing holding apart two sliding metal plates

He walked unnoticed to the opposite curb
    To a busy sidewalk
Where each worried of the calamities
    That might befall their children

He thought of the time when
    He stepped with bare feet on a bat
        In the dark bedroom of the farmhouse
            Where he grew up
And heard it skitter off, squeaking with insult

He had wondered how to figure the odds
    The inconvenience of rabies shots, the cost and the trouble
        Versus the risk of a disease with no cure

His son worried about the bat
    Waiting in the freezing compartment for testing
"Think of it this way," his son said. "The bat is dead,
    And you just might die."

THE OLD PIANO

Bright lights – a slap – a hug to a warm breast
A snuggle in a blanket

All contrived
All invented
Perhaps my life is all invented

I said "Mama" when I was two.
I remember well – or I was told

Walled in a crib
Four legs set in pans of water
To foil the bed bugs
Who close down hotels – as I see as I walk up 8th Avenue
Remembering, as I pass 41st Street

At 40th Street I saw a man, limping
Or was it 39th

Where I passed a child in a stroller
I remember that I had to walk – no wheels back then

Or hold my mother's hand
Where was my father's hand
Behind his back
Or over his typewriter

I found a frog when I was 4
I touched a fish when I was 5
A sunfish from the lake that my grandfather caught

He made us sling shots
And we sang as he played the old piano.

RELIQUARIES (AND PRECISION)

The center will remain empty
A reliquary with no bone
    A saint-less sanctuary

Except, perhaps, for an idea
    A thought, a formula
Giving, in those mathematically exact terms
The age of the universe
The speed that the second star in Orion's belt
    A billion star galaxy really
Is moving away from us
Or is it we, who flee from them
    In parsecs per macro-millennia

Do we care, as long as the figure is precise
    The correct answer that we could get in math class
The sum of twos equals four
It is clear, there is no room for equivocation
    No almosts, nearlys, or abouts

While, in the next room
Those muddling writers taking an English test
Can only fumble around the page
Leaving the answer in the midst of a swirl of words
    As in the eye of a hurricane

I'm afraid that
    Nature is a poet
        Not a mathematician
For show me some precision in my garden
Tell me the weight of a black hole
Is that a or b or c
    Or none-of-the-above

You may place, in the center of your reliquary
    The object of choice
        Your faith
Or a piece of your God
But mine will remain empty
A page where books can be written
Or calculations taken to their perfect conclusion

SEX IS SILLY

Ah the mistakes that lovers make
All the chances that they take
There's one thing that they always miss
The important role of silliness

Let's take off pants and skirts and socks and lie in bed together
Then let's pretend it's nothing new and talk about the weather
Then tickle, stroke and pit-i-pat, and slide beneath the covers
Take your time, explore and rhyme, you'll become the best of lovers

Sex is silly, sex is cool, but sex can make you furious
The problem is that your approach is really much too serious

Making love is rather droll, but lovers tend to frown
You think you cannot laugh at sex, but you're acting like some clowns
You're lying in the rumpled bed, one on top, one upside down
You're bouncing, bumping, groping, and scriggling around

What you really do when making love I'm sure you'll never tell me
But what naked people do in bed, is really rather silly

On the edge of the schoolyard
On the lowest level
Where the 8th graders were allowed to play
There was a swamp.
Guarded by low trees, enmeshed in vines
Dark, even during morning recess
With stagnant pools masquerading as mossy ground
Growing skunk cabbages
And islands of sharp grass

When the throw was too high to first base
The soft mud would grab our softball
And give it up, reluctantly
With a sucking sound
And we'd run, leaping back to the hard packed ball field
Our footprints closing up behind us

In class
A slight swamp odor about me
I studied the charts of the solar system
So well-ordered, with spheres and orbits
A clean ring around Saturn
All held together by unseen strings of gravity
I thought, there's too much order in this universe
The diagrams don't mesh
With the swamp that is my mind

I've read
That 90% of the mass of the universe is missing
It's called the Dark Matter
It must be found, or the formulas will remain incomplete
And one cannot choose between smooth expansion
Or an oscillation, from pinpoint to forever
And back

I think that space is a thick soup
Stuffed with the waste of the past
Woven with tendrils of thought
A morass of invisible dark matter
Planets, suns and galaxies float
In an ocean with no surface
Warm, covering, confining, pressing
Against our eyes

If the moon were picked up
The hole left in the ether
Would slowly fill with the warm dark mud

(My Bedroom Ceiling)

The spiders gather
Where the top of the wall meets the ceiling
A good spot to trap mosquitoes
That buzz warnings in my ear
I look up at the constellations
Formed by the cracks in the plaster
And survey from above
Winding streams and roads
A land bounded by the window blinds
And the ocean of my brother's sleep-breathing

When my mother finalized the rituals
Turned off the light at the top of the stairs
The ceiling faded as the music rose
I was set free to take a seat
In my own planetarium
Centered on the giant ant
Large and black and metal-plated
Dented and scarred
The skin of a beast
Calibrated to figure angles
To the sun
To the moon
And to the bend in the road
Where my grandfather's car turned out of sight
And we stopped waving

Now look here, young fellow
Speaks Galileo Galilei
Watch closely how the red one changes its place
From night to night
A motion that appears
In the asymmetry of scales
Written by scientists and oracles and
Priests that stare into the sun

He convinced small boys
That God was one with the creature
That hides beneath the bed

With my coat buttoned
In the style of the day
And my watch set on time
I wave, but the giant ant is silent
It cares not a whit
If we cheer the boxer's bloody hands
Nor cries
If I miss the yellow bus

POEM FOR ALBERT EINSTEIN

I'm walking forward, and speeding backwards
A passenger moving to the rear of a fast-moving train
Under a warm perpetually exploding bomb
On a slipping and sliding unattached plate
A headlong careening trip through space
Causing red and yellow leaves
                    To glow in the autumn
                                        In the evening
When the clock slowly approached the streetcar
Until the patent clerk could be seen
                    Thinking.
Gentle man, he wrote love letters
                    And stripped us to our minds
He thanked my mother for her offer of a ride
                    But said he'd rather walk
And we sped away

CHIARO-SCURO

West

In the temporary limestone shade I set up an easel
Of oiled chestnut and brass fittings
With three legs to foil the shifting ground

I need only primary colors here
Red for ground, blue for sky
These cliffs can be squeezed onto a canvas board
Into a homily
"If only people would love one another, then..."
"If only government would get off our backs..."

The problem, chosen people, is
There's too much space here
I am the first to walk on this gravel
Where tastes are raw and distinctions clear
And time has not refined the sand
200 years of strata laid bare, no privacy
No place to hide my heathen mind

East

I stand my easel on an Appalachian slope
Each foot nestled in soft maternal soil
The paint box is heavy in the grass
Thalo green, yellow ochre,
Colbalt blue and burnt sienna
Colors for the chaos of a Kittatinny meadow

Saxifrage and the clock have turned these rocks into fine aged sand
Arranged by Emerson and Thoreau into thickets of ideas
That shield the hiding child
Nature governs with a permissive hand
Over many hellos, and no unrubbed shoulders
A meadow built of a thousand mistakes

In the swamp, my paintings hang on mossy trees
And thrill to the praise of the cicadas

DRIVING TO FLORIDA

(Or, how Euclidean theory gave way to quantum mechanics)

When the Autumnal equinox
Shakes the robes off the trees that circle our house
And the outside moves indoors
We close the windows around a shrinking universe
It is time to go to Florida

Following a line from the top to the bottom of our frayed map
Taped at the edges
Folded around the route
And held upside down to point in the right direction
We drive south

After three days in my back-seat cocoon
I'll emerge as a new kid
In the sixth grade
So, while time is at the wheel
I gaze out the side window, and hold
With my eyes
A fixed point beside the car
I float easily over low fields
Then jump, dodge, and bounce over posts, trees, and
Barns left too close to the road

Hypnotized by the miles,
My parallel self becomes still and calm
Stationary in the air
While the rocks, signs, and trees race and scramble
Headlong backwards
Running to our empty house
To play with the toys I left behind

Traveling to the sun, through the Flatland of our map
Along US 1, because
            Odd numbers run North-South
We will spend the winter in Florida
And search for shells on an empty beach
            Before it becomes Cape Canaveral
                        Later, Cape Kennedy
And dig in the sand, where
            Rockets will roar, and leave lingering vapor trails
At right angles to the earth
            Connecting the sand with the sky

On these winter trips,
I never know, with much certainty,
            Our exact speed
                        Or precise location
Which seem to vary, depending upon which observer
            My mother or my father
                        Is looking at the map
But we probably are on the right road
And we probably will reach Jacksonville
            By tomorrow   (according to my watch)
                        Night   (on this side of the Earth)

THE WRISTWATCH

I don't remember who gave me my first wristwatch
No doubt a Christmas present
I do remember that it was made of shiny metal
And it was thick, and the glass curved upwards over the dial
Like the front of a spaceship
It was as heavy as a stone
And I thought my arm would stretch
Or I'd end up walking with a tilt
Like my father, who fell at the age of five
He was thirty-eight before he knew his neck was broken

So many cautions, so many fantasies lurked beneath the glass bubble
At school it said:
"You're late for class
"Only twenty more minutes till recess
"It takes thirty-three minutes for my desktop to move through the shadow of the window pane

At the dentist it calculated
An average of two minutes between drillings
And the difference between normal minutes and the "He doesn't need Novocain" minutes

The two hands spoke to me in hieroglyphics
Signaling like the flag man on an aircraft carrier
To speed up or slow down
At night it ticked against my ear
In rhythm with my heart

When I was bored
I would pull the stem
Turn the burred knob
And set the sun to spinning
For if the back were pried off
Inside worked a tiny orrery
Circling paths, large and small
Each linked to the next
In a connected system of planets

A universe with a clear purpose, and a God
Who would spin insanely
                    When I reset the time

The thin second hand could not be stopped
                    As it stepped smoothly around the circle, along the rim
Although, sometimes if one looked very closely
                    Its motion would slow, almost imperceptibly
                    A metaphysical shudder

Quickly I would wind it tightly
Or sometimes, in class
                    I'd wind it to defy the teacher
Hoping the girl across the aisle
Would notice

My watch was not waterproof
                    It stayed on the shore while I swam
I knew not how long it took
                    To swim to the raft in the middle of the pond
Lying on the warm boards,
                    I'd look back to the picnic table
                                        For a glimpse of the abandoned machine
                                                            Faithfully counting out
parcels of time

Squinting to see the disc
                    As I would gaze through space to observe a super nova
An interstellar explosion
                    Light from a ring of gas
                    Buffeted by a storm of particles
A solar system in birth or death
Events of a few hundred thousand years before we were born
                    Colliding before my eyes

I cannot see my watch

But only images of its past
As it was some microscopic time ago
Before each second arrives, another is born
Two times, exiting at the same instant
Competing to be the "right time"

Einstein had discovered
That my watch was not the same as any other
It kept my private time
Finding and losing hours and minutes
To use, to save, or to ignore

Around me, on the streets of New York
Walked other clocks and watches
Big pocket watches, slow lumbering grandfather clocks, quick digitals
Important pendants, albatrosses around the neck
Some with watches so rich and jeweled
As though time would care
And John, the drunk, unseen
With time as slow as mud

Each keeping step in their own fourth dimension
Old movies walking by
Knowledge is the beginning of loneliness
The other swimmers have moved on
Leaving me with faded pictures
Asleep in old photo albums
The other swimmers have moved on
Leaving behind the pictures I see, only their memories
I was liberated
From the restrictions and bounds of chronology

My watch died of a broken spring
Well before its time

THE ORRERY

In red mahogany and brass, an orrery
Etched with evenly spaced radiants
Clear and ordered markings of the universe
Replacing the void left when they broke the crystal spheres
And took us from the center
Each spherical planet moving with regard for the others
Night to day, winter to summer
Eclipses and conjunctions nicely planned
An elegant machine made to be seen from the outside
Giving the lie to its totality
I, looking in, am no longer alone
For beside me floats the Voyager, sent into space
Still working without complaint
Or trace of acrophobia
It speaks to the small brass ball
There, on the third ring
The one with blue and green
Tracing the path in reverse, I shrink into the display
To planet, to moon, to mountain
Once Gulliver, now a Lilliputian
This beautiful symmetry allows me to move from universe to universe
Passing electron planets and their proton sun
Until I return to watch the model
Standing on turtles, all the way down
Where I can, with Archimedes' lever
And a touch of left English
Bounce Mars off the sun
Ending with a gentle kiss of Earth

A THUNDERSTORM IN THE COUNTRY

I counted to one
One – only one
Before the crash came
The bolt hit a tree
(I hope it was a tree)
Outside the window
Eleven hundred feet up the hill
The flash cut the sky
Reflected off the kitchen wall
Left a jagged streak in my eye
I began to count, one two three
I had only reached one
When the thunder boomed
With a force that shook the house
Eleven hundred feet per second
The sound raced as fast as it could
Towards me, chasing the flash, far ahead
Only a second, but the flash was already in Netcong,
Or speeding through Newton
Or, at the speed of light, in outer space
The thunder, the crash
Trying to catch up
But forever left behind
As we are
Forever left behind
As the world races on
Struggling to catch up with the universe

LEFT HEMISPHERE

The drawing is unfinished
A figure, flat to the wall, cannot look out
I draw an eye, only one
On the right side
It stares
Then frowns
And speaks
"Art is a lie"

We began to fall when Newton
Moved the earth towards the apple
He stole all centers
And scattered the stars like spilt marbles
Then Einstein messed with space and time
And let in the insane
Who, alone, could read the clocks
But it is for Jesus that I painted the eye
In profile
Left the back side for the devil
And set the clock at half past twelve
So they could ring the bells on time
And know that proof of guilt is innocence claimed
This crime remains
And the witch
And I
And the drunks on
36th Street
Know that tomorrow
I will hold the key

The madman is the mayor
When the calendar is redone
The right eye winks, it's on my left
And sends the papers on.

PICTURE FRAME

The window has square edges
It defines the picture beyond
It defines what I see
Tells a story, tells a tale, sings a song

Move my head a little to the left
The canvas has been changed
The scene that I was watching
Is no longer still the same

Every view has a frame—a limit
As a museum masterpiece
Shift it right or left or up or down
You're living in a different place

One's mind creates the edges
Defines what you will see
The world is a different place
When shifted five degrees

We make sure to censure
Keep thoughts outside the frame
You cannot include it all
You'd clearly go insane

Make my own exclusions
I know that I am right
Create my own illusions
The rest is out of sight

We live inside a picture frame
On someone else's gallery
We bump against the edges
They've built a wall around us
Tis curious what they think they see
Admirers look upon us
Envious of our beauty
They think they'd like to join us

We remain imprisoned
Inside the picture frame

AGE CAN BE BEAUTIFUL

I was one when I was young
I was two a year beyond
Three followed rather quickly
Then four, who knows, now I'm all grown

I've been hanging all around
For longer than it seems
I will not say the number
But it's no longer in the teens

My mind is still a teen-ager
But the body has gone elsewhere
My thoughts, naïve and childish
But I may die next year

Growing older, hair is grayer
But there's still a place for me
So many people – the street is thriving
I'm here but I am not seen

It's not so easy, not so simple
To shove me out the door
I'll hang around, in the background
For a few more years or more

Age is very beautiful
One knows so many things
But age is very fleeting
Soon the church bell rings

Reserve for me a comfortable seat
In the far, far upper tier
They'll say nice things about me
Things I'd really like to hear

Save me from the shelter
Offered by friends
That lulls the brain and sedates the scorpions
With warmth and scheduled certainty
They
Confusing art with beauty
Offer condolences

Save me from shameless nature
Colors straight from the factory
Where beauty thrives, even within the dried hornet
Caught between windows for the winter
God help me, faced with a sunset
Over Utah's red cliffs
Paint this or leave no trace
Rather keep me in a room at night
With white, white paper
And a pen with the blackest ink
To scratch an epitaph

Ideas are not pretty
They are ugly things, forced onto the page
Squeezed from a tube
Dripping around the edges
Of a careless sentence
Be careful
Art is what you throw away
When the picture is finished and framed
The ideas are left in the ink stains
On your cuffs
After the book is published
And praised

And death is an alarm clock
With no face

VANISHING POINTS

(A definition of my paintings)

As the millennium approaches
I draw landscapes
Vanishing points shift
Consistent with the probabilities
that remain of once precise science

Boxes, bones and chess pieces
Arranged on a platform
Free-standing on a plane
Testify to the affairs
Of scientists and priests

A black and white palette
With overlapping grays
Panders to a fear of nuance
While variables fill the gaps
In unbalanced equations

A flat horizon
Determines your height
Suggesting that the earth is round
Returning to the point
Where you stand

Shadows
Place us in a solar system
Where every world rotates
Around every other
Phantoms slide along the ground

Perspective
Shows us where we might have been
Or could be later on
Glory to the viewer
Rather than the Lord

As for time
The most misunderstood dimension
Yesterday's lines are left un-erased
To compete with today's definition
Of clarity

MEDITATIONS ON A DRAWING

Shade in the desert is hard-edged
　　　　And scared
It hides at noon under overhangs
　　　　Sculpted and left behind by water and wind
I scrape a line to divide light and shadow
　　　　And another, as the retreat
Leaves a parallel series lying in the sun
　　　　To mark a million mile journey

In a two-room school house
　　　　The shadow of the window's edge
　　　　Is as sharp as limestone
I placed the point of my pencil
　　　　On the edge of the shadow
　　　　　　　　On my desk
　　　　And watched as it crept towards the ink well
If I could hold the line still
　　　　Between thumb and forefinger
The earth would freeze in its orbit
The clock would stop

During the eclipse
Noncommittal crescents scatter under maple trees
The birds are quiet
　　　　Summer colors soft
In the yard
　　　　Behind the house
　　　　　　　　Up the road
　　　　　　　　　　　　Where my cousins play

In 'real life,' I argue against absolutes
And fear the comfort of moral certainty
On paper, I like precision
Drawn in crisp black and white
With many borders
Clear, sharp-edged ambiguity
With no center
For where is the middle of the field
By the brook
Near the forest
By the rocks
I can whiplash this natural painting
By rolling my eyes
As for scale
Each mark on the ruler is in thousandths
The coastline is made of fractal miniatures
And within them, more

The footless fellow
The one I draw
The plumb bob
The pointer on a metric scale
Feels quite at home in these uncertain surroundings
He can set his watch with miles per hour
And amaze his friends with forecasts of the past.

He looks into the inked scene around him
Or turns, ninety degrees to the surface
To escape Flatland
He hangs onto the frame
Casts a shadow over his own likeness
Observes and is observed,
A cosmic voyeur

Anonymous in the desert
I am forever one step removed
With no stroke of the brush
A print
Facing neither in nor out
The words read backwards from this side
The flesh is hidden in the formulas of creation
The heart is of cold aluminum
I use photographs, and etchings
Made only of contrasts
Two dimensional, and without eyes

In my overlapping perspectives
The Tower of Pisa rises straight towards the heavens
From its site on the slope of a hill
While Brunelleschi searches
For a spot to set his easel.

The lawn grows faster now
The wisteria reaches out to grab me
As I scramble off the porch
There used to be a path between the porch and the forsythia
But now it's grown over

The catalpa blooms
And the bear ignores me
He's more interested in the sickle pear tree

My head is hurting
My back is hurting
Or is it my neck that hurts more
And I need two pillows to make the cane chair comfortable

As the sky darkens, evening threatens
Jupiter will be out soon to peek through the thin clouds
He tells the stars when it's ok to follow

The weed whacker is heavier now
Electric, with a hundred feet of orange cord
Winding back to the studio

Another hundred feet of cord and I could plug my brain in
And still walk the length of the lawn
If I could adjust the power,
Change the voltage to jar the thoughts
Maybe zap the one about standing on the edge of that high bridge

But who is that guy
Who wants to unplug me
Pull the cord, leave the socket
Do I know him, or her

No power is in—power is out
Listen to what I say, I tell the dentist
I said to the doctor

I said to the man spread gentleman who sits beside me
In the subway car

And I'm embarrassed to look at the knees, the thighs
Of the woman, the lady, sitting across from me
Who is plugged in
Do those ear buds send signals to her brain
To censor thoughts of the bridge
Or is she dull normal

Oh to be dull normal
Keep those fantasies in check
And remember I have to buy some milk
And some half and half
And some crispy baked chocolate cookies
That I can eat tomorrow at lunch, with a beer

And forget the news, the news of the day
That I hope is just of the day
And prefer to feel today's pain
In my neck
In my back
In my mind
And to remember there will
Always be
A tomorrow

THANK YOU

Thank you,   thank you
For reading my poems
Or any one will do
I feel your vision
I can write again, like I used to
Find some words,   line 'em up,   put 'em in a row

Put 'em in a heap,   make 'em rhyme,   make 'em weep
Put 'em in a pile,   take your time,   make 'em smile

Poems live on,   after the poet flies away
You've allowed me,   to stay another day
And scribble down thoughts,   make sense of them later
I've chosen the words, I'm the creator

So thank you for allowing my pen to reveal
A poem, a new poem
Perhaps you
Should write
A few

SONNETS

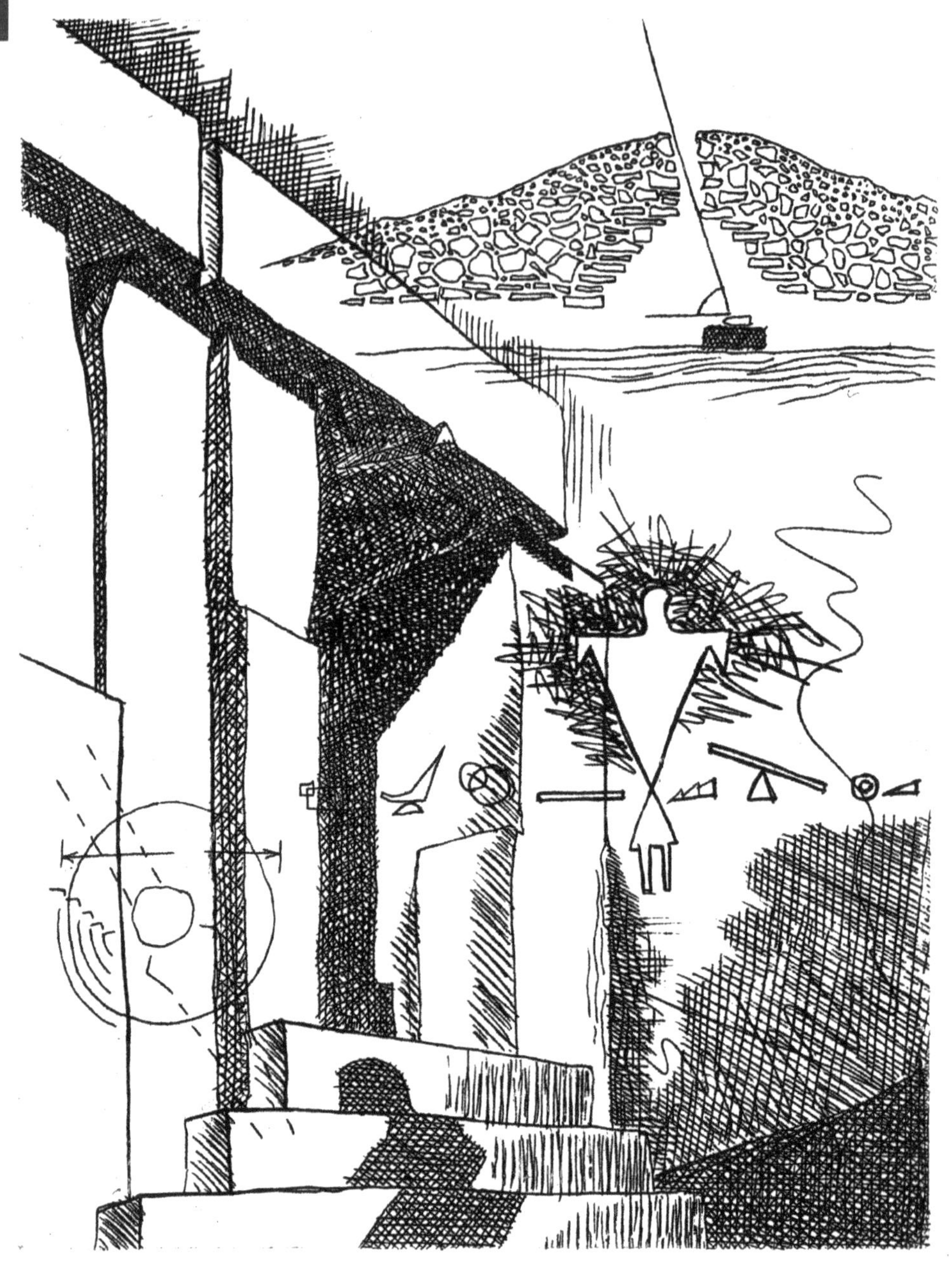

TIS WILL

(Upon receiving a faxed Shakespeare sonnet from a friend and the last six lines were lost)

Tis Will, surprise, who speaks from printed page
And sends his words, by line to me, from you
But not with ease in this 'lectronic age
The wrath of wires will not permit him through

In sonnet olde, awaken thoughts of REM
And artists found the first surrealist light
The Bard pervades the Net, he lives again
To see his verse cut down by trivial might

Words fly to ether, return to cyber speak
A sea of senseless points, a nightmare wrought
With a o l dot com resound, I think
Words made and made again without a thought

For number forty three, although tis great
He rhymed, I fear, with lines of more than eight

YOU THINK I WROTE JUST ONE

OK OK you think I wrote just one
To write again is only in my dreams
That thoughts will end just as the thought's begun
The truth will wake and silence is its means

But being one who rarely finds success
Whose work's dismissed, too full of black and white
One compliment becomes a full day's feast
And puts the brain in gear in dark of night

Good fax will mock with long and whitish tongue
New words to prove the fish was not a fluke
Know well that when the active deed is done
Inertia's quick to speak a harsh rebuke

So fast, look now, to sight creative breath
For noon-time nap will soon renew its death

CORPORATE TASKS

Why is one doomed with skills for corporate tasks
Dull dollars rule, the truths they speak stand false
No gold is giv'n, no thanks for questions asked
Pursuits I love are pleasures for the lost

Work time is grist to feed these epitaphs
Waste fuels each line of this ongoing joke
But I'm the butt, for those who cannot laugh
Are growing rich, whilst I am growing broke

Intestines feel no nurture in romance
And pockets sigh in hopes of treasures big
Alas, good poets write about the dance
While bacon sleeps untouched within the pig

Let's plan, forsooth, to market by the pound
Such unknown Shakespeare fax that I have found

CRUEL WORDS

Oh my, oh my, oft-times cruel world will jest
With souls off guard, perhaps to bring a smile
To those with pens who write to beat their breast
And view the play while standing in the aisle

Sharp humor's lost on takers of the punch
Lines laced with wit will stripe my shielded core
I would be charmed to watch this daily crunch
From first tier center, row three, seat number four

Act one's own critic, observe but never feel
Control the pen, let ink create false flower
Red blood flows from the brush when art's surreal
Revise the book, and hide between the covers

But ruse backfires, as I observe my day
Reviews I write, read crueler than the play

SLY TRICKSTER

Sly trickster in the brain is back again
To wield his wand, and conjure ancient scripts
Performances begin at three A M
When maestro takes command, as reason slips

Arriving late, I miss the overture
T'was played before, confusion comes and grows
Of right or wrong or nothing am I sure
The humor stings, I have forgot my clothes

Acts start, scenes pass, the plot proceeds unclear
While actor's words are swords that cut fresh wounds
Upon the frail pretensions that I bear
Throughout the play, begun when I left home

But envy not, those with no dreams at night
And treasure fear, it prods you to awake

THE SPICE OF LIFE

(Upon reading that acetic acid was "found" in Sagittarius B2, 25,000 light years away from Earth.)

The captain raised his glass, searched for a land

Rich in clove, mace, nutmeg, an older place

On Earth's reverse, where at the ocean's end

All ships and men fall into outer space

As ancients could not see 'round nature's curve

Much faith was placed in versions of the truth

But history's not writ til we observe

The light that brings its footprints into view

Now far beyond the galaxies we find

New meanings are revealed in spectral lists

From Sagittarius, far back in time

Not life, but vinegar, it seems, exists

Perhaps around another bend unseen

Lie lettuce leaves to make the salad green

THE DENTIST'S CHAIR

Imagination serves when ether fails
To act upon the aches that plague and irk
One dreams of routes through Venice's canals
Where silver fills the voids of daily work

The pearly gates of youth gleamed forth so bright
To blind the truth, but now each time my grin
Shines out to dazzle ladies dressed in white
They're not impressed, for they are looking in

Tis not too thoughtful using mind's resource
To replace wisdom, bite and beauty lost
From gross neglect, or taken so by force
We won the brush with death, but oh the cost

Rue not the wayward ways that sent us there
The mind must float above the dentist's chair

THE BIG COMMISSION

Oh my, I'm broke again; sculpture, God knows
Has not the wherewithal to fill the table
My children suffer shame from wearing clothes
That advertise their plight with unknown labels

But lo, I have perhaps struck gold. I'm asked
To build a fountain large and beautiful
Green corporate dollars, waiting there at last
If only I can bow to all the rules

But how, the jury that decides this trial
Believes the artist must invent new forms
To prove their love of art, yet all the while
Stay true to Disney's laws and Jesse's norms

Oh Hell, I think I'll quit and just go fishin'
And there perchance I'll catch a big commission

PRICE UPON REQUEST

I've set upon a quest, most difficult

To find art's cutting edge, the guard avant

An update of my taste will sure result

With knowledge of what rich collector's want

First study closely every press release

Then check upon the gallery's pedigree

Learn from the text that's posted by each piece

But price, of course, is finally the key

At openings, white wine to quench the thirst

Created by unchallenged gallery walls

I'll give you my corrected thoughts, but first

Excuse me please, I feel that nature calls

The answer to the query what is art

It must include at least one body part

ON NET SONNET

(By a has-been poet)

I've flirted in the past with rhyme and verse
Which do not seem, in retrospect, too lame
But new attempts have waked the silence curse
Well known to all who dabble in art's game

A poet finds no path, just open sea
To chart a course across the void, one might
Admire the jumps and bites of every flea
Pursuing life without a goal in sight

For in the welts left by these rude insects
The secret: fail, but fail abundantly
Create and leave behind, mountains of drek
Wherein a new idea may hidden be

I write and leave it to biographers
To see if any art, perchance, occurred

CHAOS THEORY

White clouds, dark smoke and waterfalls, and swings

With crazy rhythms call for mention in

Great halls where Nobel-minded science kings

Dissect clean billiard balls in action, when

Laboratory windows shake, rain gusts

Add random noise, results are skewed, ignored

By minds who wait the passing storm, and thus

Hear not the clap of butterfly wings, that roared

Absorbing laws of nature all the while

Drops kick and spin, a gleeful chaos dance

But from this brew shines my reflected smile

A speck of calm defying laws of chance

From order there comes chaos, the surprise is

The order in the chaos that arises

(On placing a sculpture, "neutrino-catcher," in an Etruscan tomb)

Good news, good news, for from on high a voice

Has spoken well, and willed to me a tomb

Why, you may ask does this make one rejoice

Only a fool receives such news sans gloom

But despair not, for neither is my fate

To be reborn, nor fall the prey to prayer

Art wins the game, I'm asked to decorate

The space where other's souls and bones be bare

The Lord gives reason it is said to life

When all that needs explaining is design

I'll place within this cave a grand device

To watch the speeding universe rewind

Thus capturing the steady beat of time

I'll find immortal rhythms without rhyme

PUFFERFISH

Written upon learning that the gene pool of the spotted green pufferfish rivals that of humans

Atop the chain of food we smugly roost
With genes, two hundred thousand to explain
The reason for our skill of symbol use,
Our languages complex, our giant brain

But wait, new research has produced
A total now of thirty thou', still less --
For recently the thou's have been reduced
To twenty, and that's just the latest guess

Problem is, there lives another beast
Whose count can match this small amount of genes
T'is not the clever chimpanzee, please meet
The pufferfish, and worse it's spotted green

So in the pool, when bitten on the toe
Remember, don't get mad, just say "hello"

DOGGEREL SONNET

Playing with the charms of lowly doggerel
A friend rose to the task, did rather well.
My early brush, alas, with doctor Will
iam Carlos Williams did not auger well

For skillful rhyme. For in his boozy voice
He argued well in poems that things came first
And in a red wheelbarrow I found the choice
To scrap the time, and dabble in free verse.

Now no standards make me hesitate
Like plates of pasta spilled, to spew out lines
And I like every would be W. B. Yeats
Use freedom to eliminate design

But secretly I'm quite a fan of doggerel
I also grew up citing Lewis Carroll

POEMS FOR THE SUMMER SOLSTICE

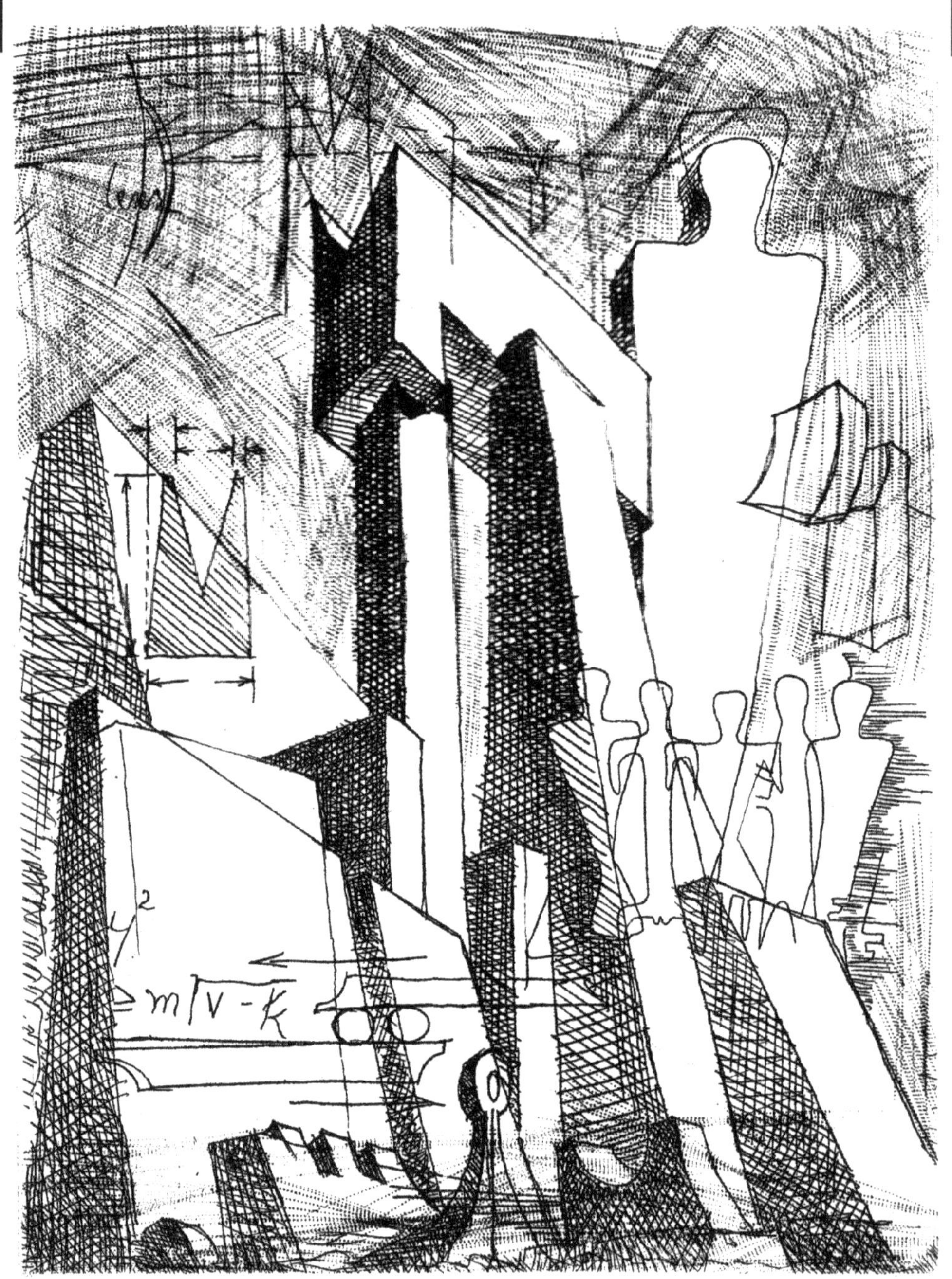

A MOVING SHADOW

When I look at the stone
Still warm from its birth
Still cold from the glacial shove
I see the carver.

Listen
You can hear the hammer strike the anvil
And on the blackboard, half erased
Is the formula for the curve
Of the arc of a falling chip

I tire from hauling this stone forty kilometers
I remember the blood, when
As a boy, I cut my foot
on the marble chips at the quarry
Where stones are now sliced
And taken to skin new towers

To this scene include a moving shadow
That charts the earth's turn
And I create a picture, that
Makes the camera blind

THE EXACT TIME

When the clock reads
Eight hours
Fifty minutes
Point three one four seconds
P. M.
Precise
To the millisecond
Plus or minus two thousand years
It's time to leave

Don't walk in the ruins after dark
When time gets fuzzy
When the builder and the visitors
Stand side by side
Sighting true north over the heel stone

IT'S RAINING ON THE SOLSTICE

The first raindrop ricochets off sandstone
Vaporizes in the desert air
The second hits the ground
Perches as a crystal ball
Rejected by the red dust
The third and fourth combine
To smooth
And soften the sharp edges
Of rocks cut to fit exactly in place
A rare storm begins at the ruins

At noon, the skies clear, the desert dries itself
Sunlight warms the southern face of the rock
While the northern back stays chilled
Shadows crawl along the edge of the circle

The clouds have passed
The storm appears to leave no trace
But now, a sunbeam touches the spiral's edge
Meanings have been changed
Their purpose muddied
And the margin of error has increased

STUNTED OAK

A stunted oak has twisted its way

Through the carved stone floor

With no respect for the temple

It slid the heel stone an inch to the left

Moved Polaris half a degree

Edged the earth from its axis

Melted glaciers

And set the forests on fire

THE TAR-PIT MACHINE

I would like to die in a tar pit
Next to a carved rock
Too large to move
My bones shall be aligned to celebrate the sky's anniversaries
The extreme points
Center lines
Eclipses and occlusions
The sun's shadow at the equinox will light my pointing finger
The socket in my skull will sight along the stone
To Polaris
Always there for comfort
Some little known bones will be aligned with distant stars
Known brightly only to their neighbors

I would like to die in a tar pit
And become a machine, with one moving part
Counting the years it takes for trees to grow into diamonds

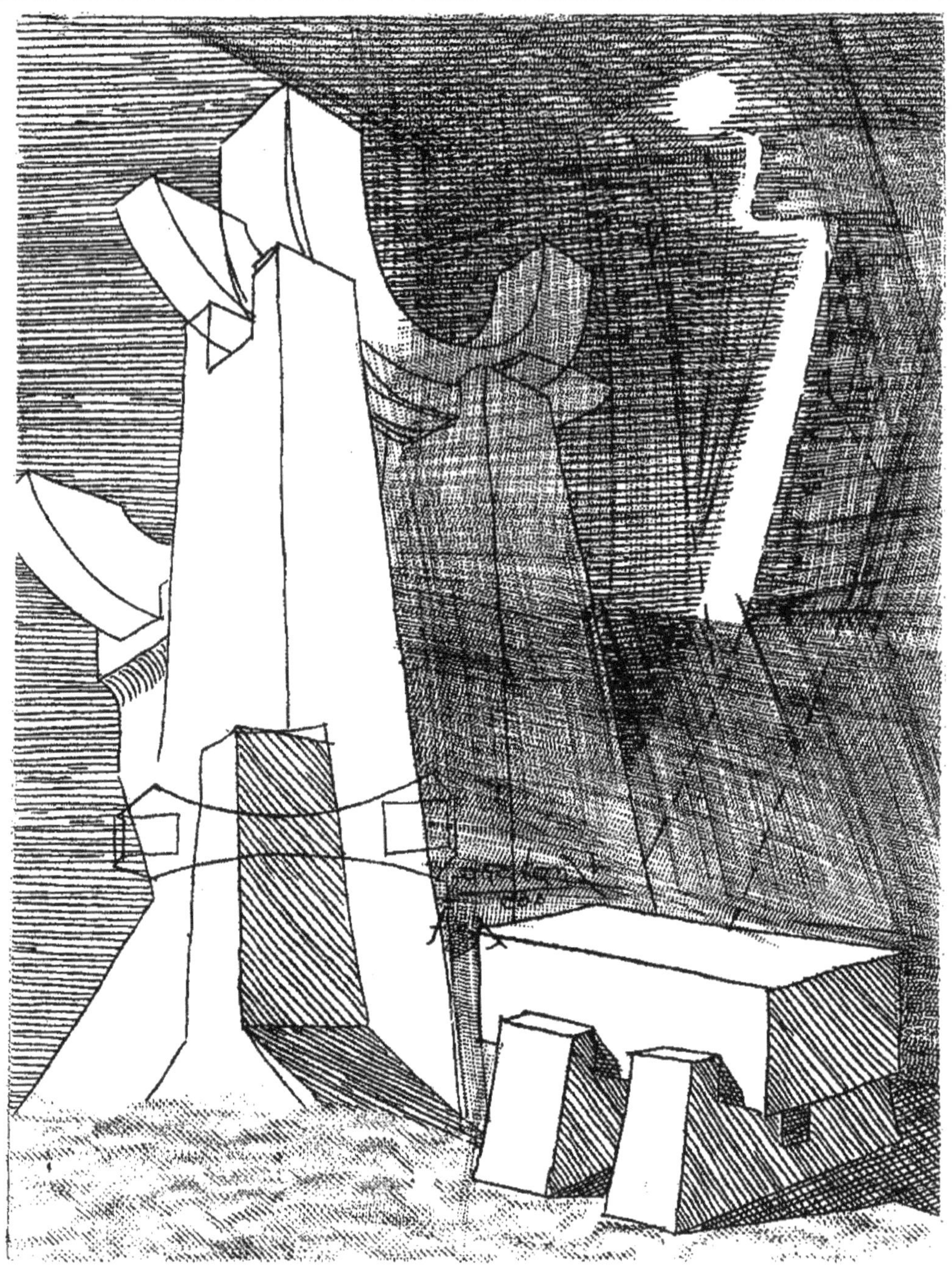

POEM FOR THE PANDEMIC

In these tough days I'd like to inspire us

And put my thoughts into a song

But what does one rhyme with coronavirus

Everything I try just goes wrong

But even worse is the word pandemic

The most un-rhymable word I've seen

As a poet I wholly condemn it

But try rhyming with COVID-19

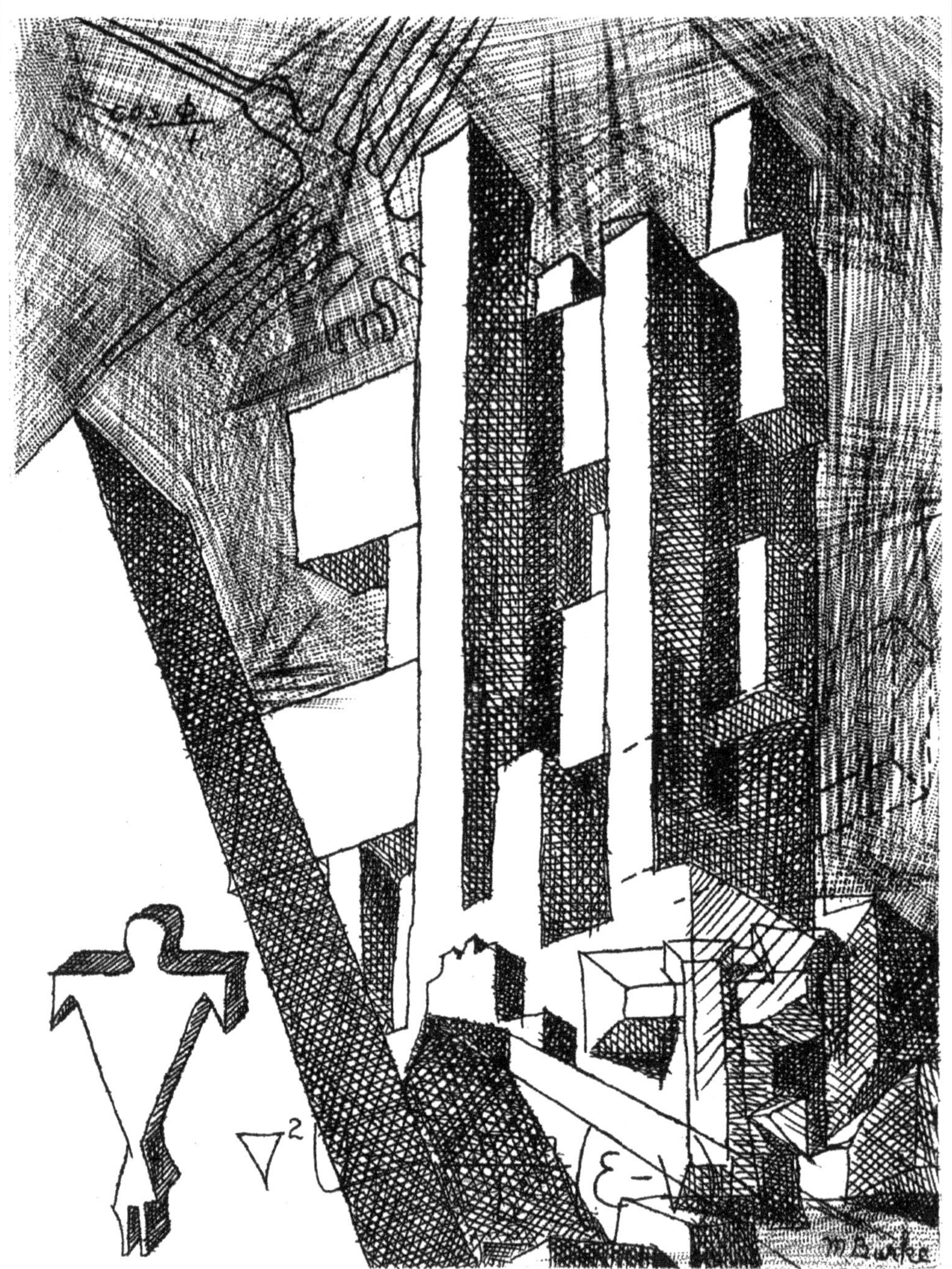

ACKNOWLEDGMENTS

"Words" first appeared in the *School of Visual Arts Magazine*, 2008 and then *The Round*, 2009.

"Perspective" first appeared in *Potomac Review*, Fall/ Winter 2002.

"Martini Tryptych" first appeared in *Journal of New Jersey Poets*, 2010.

"Reliquaries (and Precision)" first appeared in the *Hunterdon Museum Catalogue*, 1995, and then *Journal of New Jersey Poets*, Spring 1996.

"Poem For Albert Einstein" first appeared in the *Celle Ligure Catalogue*, 1992.

"Driving to Florida" first appeared in *Journal of New Jersey Poets*, Winter 1998.

"The Orrery" first appeared in the *Academy of Sciences Catalogue*, 199?.

"Vanishing Points" first appeared in the *ASYL Gallery Catalogue*, 1999.

"Meditations on a Drawing" first appeared in *Journal of New Jersey Poets*, Autumn 1994.

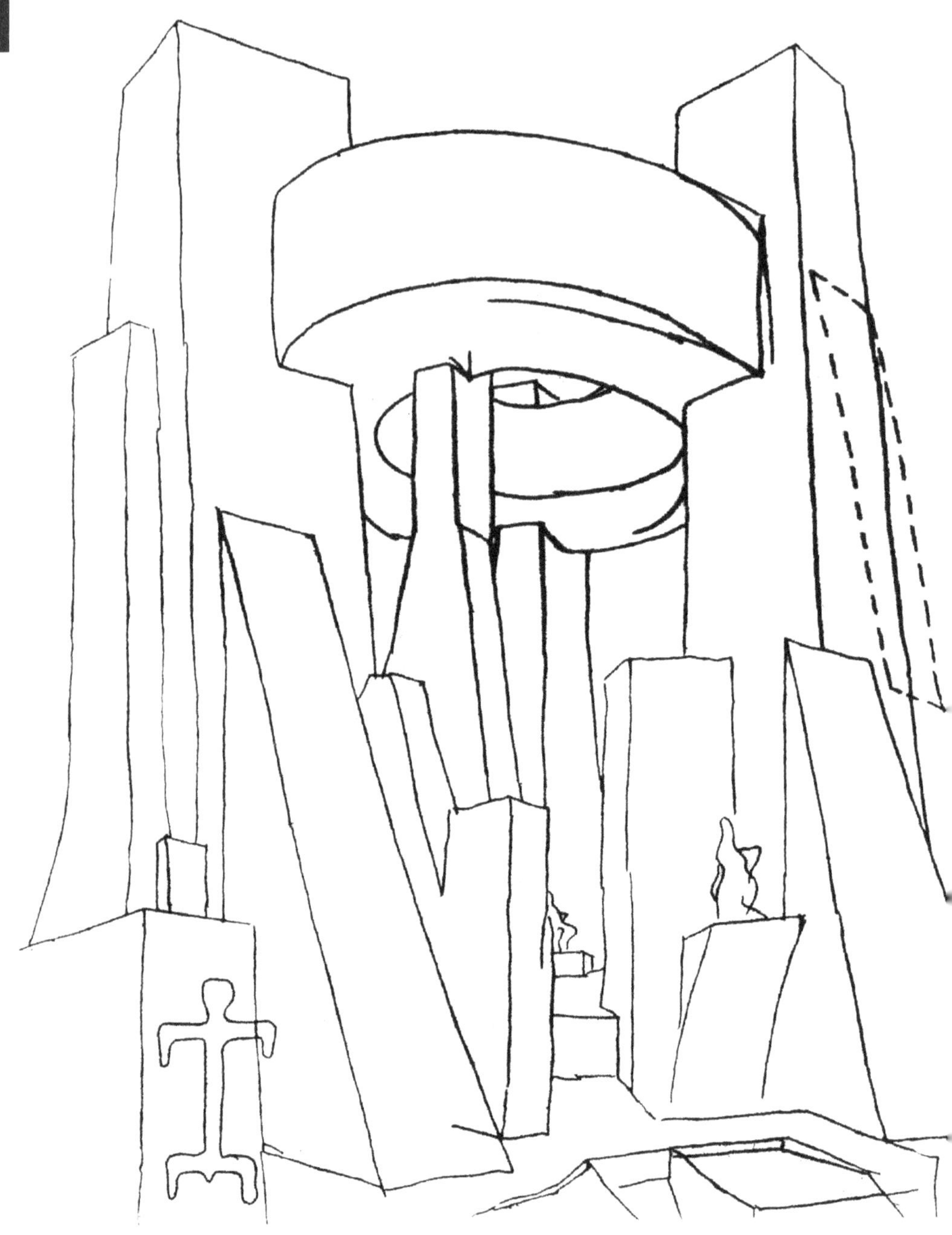

ABOUT THE AUTHOR

Michael Burke has traveled through a number of careers since he graduated from college. The first was as an astronomer, working at observatories in the U.S., Hawaii, and Iran. He then went back to school to obtain a Master's Degree in City Planning. He worked in New York City's Planning Department and later became an Assistant Professor at Columbia's Graduate School of Architecture and City Planning. Michael changed direction again when he found a loft in Soho and began to paint. He has been an artist for more than thirty years—painting, drawing, and lately producing aluminum books and sculpture. He has exhibited his work extensively in the U.S., Japan, and Europe. As a fiction writer, Michael is the author of the Johnny "Blue" Heron adventure trilogy, consisting of *Swan Dive* (2009), *Music of the Spheres* (2011), and *Out of Mind* (2014).

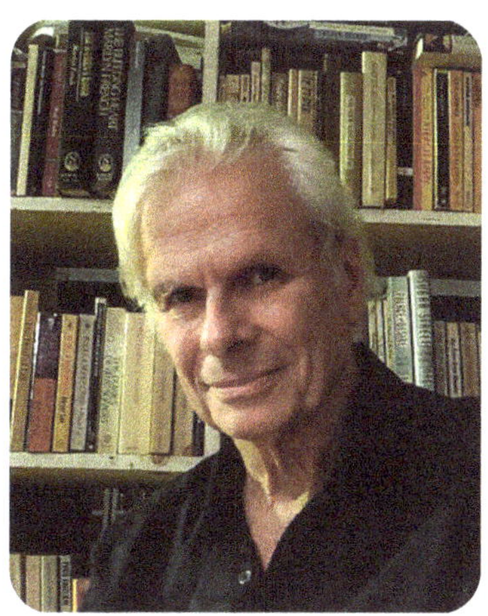

MICHAEL BURKE

www.ingramcontent.com/pod-product-compliance
Lightning Source LLC
LaVergne TN
LVHW052355100826
845147LV00013B/844

9781643171876